Estamos Aquí

Poems by Migrant Farmworkers

Translated by Janine Pommy Vega

Edited by
Sylvia Kelly
Bob Holman
Marjorie Tesser

Bowery Books
Bowery Poetry Series #4

YBK Publishers, New York

The workshops which produced the poems in this collection were funded through the New York State Council on the Arts' Literature program as a part of the Geneseo Migrant Center's CAMPS (Creative Artists Migrant Program Services) Literature program.

Cover art and graphics by Eva McKendry
Cover photograph by Athesia Benjamin

Estamos Aquí: Poems by Migrant Farmworkers

Copyright © 2007
by Bowery Arts & Science, Ltd.

All rights reserved
Including the right of reproduction in whole or in part in any form

ISBN-13: 978-0-9790972-3-2
ISBN-10: 0-9790972-3-1

Library of Congress Control Number: 2007934479

YBK Publishers, Inc.
39 Crosby Street
New York, NY 10013

Manufactured in the United States of America

ver 07-09

Bowery Books is the imprint of
Bowery Arts & Science, Ltd.,
a 501(c) (3) non-profit cultural organization,
and are published in affiliation with YBK Publishers, Inc.,
whose publisher, Otto Barz, is the inspiration for this series.
With thanks to Bill Adler.

This publication is made possible with public funds from the New York State Council on the Arts, a State agency.

Contents

Introduction

You would never guess by the Dow Jones Industrial Average, or the millions made and lost daily on the New York Stock Exchange, that the biggest actual export of a tangible commodity from New York State is farm produce. In the rolling hills and glacial plains of Western New York it is summer again, and the crops are growing. The migrant workers have returned to tend the produce that feeds this nation.

All of them speak Spanish; a few speak English. All of them share an abiding love of their homeland, and the friends and family they left—many of whom are dependent on the money sent back weekly to the tiny towns and rural villages. Laboring from sun-up to sundown, the workers are married to the produce of a foreign land. They take it personally. As one man said: "Of all the places I have harvested crops in the last twenty years—Florida, North Carolina, New Jersey, New York—I like best the Pine Barrens of New Jersey. Why? Because of the blueberry bushes. I don't reach up, I don't bend down. They are exactly my height—they are easy to pick."

A creative writing workshop with migrant farm workers begins for us in the late afternoon—five or six o'clock, after the work is done—with the long drive across Western New York. In the wide open spaces south of Rochester and as far west as Buffalo are vegetable, livestock, and dairy farms—all manned by hundreds of migrant workers with rarely a shred of legal paperwork. One worker said it best: "It's very simple. You cannot stop a river." And that's what it is—a river of human beings drawn north by our economy's need for their arms and legs, backs and hands. And by their own need to send money home to improve the standard of living for the whole family. A significant portion of the GNP of Mexico is the stream of money orders home from the farms up north.

In August the weather is just beginning to promise a breeze around six or seven; frequently we get a gorgeous sunset. We arrive at the converted motel, or the whitewashed barracks, or the barn converted into bunk bed bivouacs, or the old two story farmhouse in drastic need of repair, or the endless array of rusting trailers, just as the sky is darkening. The men have almost all eaten and showered. Eighty-five per cent of migrant farm workers are men, or boys pretending to be men so they can work, too.

Most Latin Americans I have met have the easy grace of accepting strangers without much fuss—no matter how unlikely they appear. Two middle-aged women, one with a white crew cut sticking straight up, the other with no Spanish but an earnest attitude filling in for words, show up on their doorstep in the dark and are immediately invited in. The trailer holds all the heat of a scorching day in its metal-boxed interior. Of course there is no air conditioning, there is no fan. I explain that we've come from the Migrant Center to work with them on writing poems, and they wave us to a place of honor on the battered couch. An open door and the window opposite create the start of a small cross breeze with waves of eager mosquitoes.

I have learned from repeated visits that if the inhabitants of a camp are all men they take turns making the tortillas and beans for the evening meal, each according to his own hometown recipe. Thus you could eat your way through all the states of Mexico by just staying long enough at one farm. If our timing is right, and the men have all eaten and showered, we have a small window of time before they will need to go to sleep. My belief is no one can live by bread alone, or by work alone: you need dreams and ideas that require imagination. You need something to ponder and reflect on before the day is over. I usually say something like that at the outset. The men generally agree.

I bring in simple writing exercises. Most of the men can read and write; I take dictation from those who can't. The exercises require the memory to kick in—what's the scariest moment you can remember? Who is the loveliest woman you've ever met? Did your grandparents tell you stories, stories from the old times? What's a moment, an experience that sticks in your mind and will never go away? The examples I use are poems written by Latin American writers or migrant workers from another year. As soon as everyone settles in on his own idea the room grows silent: only the sound of pens scratching on paper; maybe the smell of pig manure wafts in from the barn.

After about twenty minutes, we each have a poem; I insist every man read his own work aloud unless he cannot. I explain I will be typing out their work, translating it into English, and getting it back to them. If they have any English at all, it would be a good way to pick up some words, since they already know what the poem says. The voices as they read aloud hold a mixture of earnestness, embarrassment, and pride, but as the reading makes its way around the room the attentiveness grows; someone might be unexpectedly touched by his own words, or another's. At the end there's a general air of satisfaction at what we shared.

I take the poems away with me to translate; I'll send them back with another teacher. Oftentimes I never see the men again. It doesn't matter. We already took a moment to contemplate some things that do matter, and mostly they're the same for everyone. What these writers share with us in this book is their food for the heart.

—Janine Pommy Vega, August 2007

Janine Pommy Vega is the author of eighteen books and chapbooks since 1968. The latest is (poetry) *The Green Piano,* A Black Sparrow Book, published by David R. Godine, May 2005. A new CD with music, *Across the Table,* will come out in 2007. Vega performs with music and solo, in English and Spanish, in international poetry festivals, museums, prisons, art centers, universities, nightclubs, and migrant workers' camps in North America, South America, and Europe. Her poetry has been translated into six languages and published in a dozen countries. A *Selected Poems* will be coming out in German in Austria in 2008; an Italian translation of *Tracking the Serpent* was published in 2007. Vega is the Director of *Incisions/Arts,* an organization of writers working with people behind bars. She has taught inside American prisons for more than twenty years.

Editor's Foreword

How books get made, a true story.

I go to *Facing Pages*, the New York State Council on the Arts' statewide gathering of literary organizations—just the sentence makes me careen—BUT in fact I love these meetings, deep camaraderie and professional disbelief, the rubby edges of government and art. This is Rochester, during the Lilac Festival, spring of '06.

One of the little wisdom walks that Kathleen Masterson and Debora Ott take the conference through is "I Got a Problem/ Solution," where the participants are invited to take the microphone and in two minutes give a specific problem (or solution) and then receive crossfire watering cans from the audience. The very first Problem was presented by Sylvia Kelly of the Geneseo Migrant Center: seems a project they had, writing workshops for migrant workers, had resulted in a book of bilingual poems, but she could find no one to print it. As editor of Bowery Books it was a great pleasure to say, "Hey, that's an easy one: Bowery Books will publish *Estamos Aquí*"—and watching the look on Sylvia's face was divine. How often does one get the chance to say "Yes"? I mean, unless you are Molly Bloom.

And the more I learned of the book the better my instincts turned out to be: the teacher/editor/translator of the book turned out to be the terrific poet and activist Janine Pommy Vega, whom I've known for approximately a million years and who is top o' the line in my book (I love that cliché!) and who was a joy to work with; the folks at Geneseo Migrant Center were all in, totally supportive, patient with the usual interminable delays; Marjorie Tesser, my associate editor, and Otto Barz, publisher at YBK, publishers of the Bowery Books imprint were totally on board, and. . . .

So here is the book, here we/nosotros are, when we are those whose bed is work, whose life is the road. The poets' names are real, but the nature of their lives makes the poets themselves phantoms. If your poems are here, contact us and we will get you a copy of the book. If you are comfortable with the idea, we could have a book party and reading at the Bowery Poetry Club. This book sets sail toward understanding and community and a new nation conceived by the same old saw of welcoming all. Here's the amazing voice of our Migrant Worker Poets, direct. They are here, and they are us.

—Bob Holman, August 2007

Estamos Aquí

Poems by Migrant Farmworkers

PARA MÉXICO

Jaime Trejo

Yo soy Mexicano, mi tierra es brava.
Palabra de hombre que no hay otra tierra
más linda y más brava que la tierra mía.
Mi orgullo es ser charro valiente
y bragado. Mi orgullo lo tengo de ser
Mexicano. México lindo y querido,
si muero lejos de ti, que digan
que estoy dormido
y que me traigan a ti.
Yo le escribo a tus volcanes,
a tus praderas y flores que son como
talismanes del amor de tus amores.
Lástima, México lindo y querido,
tan lejos de Dios y tan cerca
de los Estados Unidos.

FOR MEXICO

Jaime Trejo

I am Mexican, my country is fearless.
On my word, there is no other country
prettier or more fearless than mine.
My pride is to be a valiant
and well-fitted horseman. The pride I have
is being Mexican. Beautiful beloved Mexico,
if I die far from you, let them say
that I am sleeping
and bring me back to you.
I write to your volcanoes,
to your meadows and flowers,
talismans of love from your loves.
Too bad, beautiful beloved Mexico,
that you are so far from God
and so near the United States.

CUANDO ME VINE

Román Belásques

Cuando me vine de mi país
que es Guatemala
yo, pensando en venir
a Estados Unidos
pensando que si yo
podría llegar aquí,
pero al mismo tiempo
pensado en mi familia . . .
Pero al mismo tiempo
dije, Ya ma voy.
Así es que estoy aquí
pero pensando en mi familia.

WHEN I CAME HERE

Román Belásques

When I came from my country
which is Guatemala
I was thinking of coming
to the United States,
thinking about whether I
could actually get here,
but at the same time
thinking of my family . . .
But at the same time
I said, I'm going now.
So it is that I am here now
thinking about my family, still.

LO PRIMERO QUE HICE

Alberto Sactic

El primero que hice era
consultar a mi esposa,
Hilda.
Le dije pues que había
muchos allá,
que había muchos Guatemaltecos
acá en los Estados,
y lo que hice fue decidir
a venirme acá.
Ella estaba de acuerdo.
En Guatemala hay muchos ladrones,
y se ganaba muy poco.
Decidí de venirme acá
por este lado.
Dejé a mi mujer y mis tres hijos
con mi familia.
Yo escribo a ella, y las cartas llegan;
sí, sé que llegan.
Fácil es regresar
pero venir acá es el problema.

THE FIRST THING I DID

Alberto Sactic

The first thing I did
was consult with my wife,
Hilda.
I said to her that there were
a lot of us there,
many Guatemalans
in the United States,
so it's okay
to go there.
She agreed with me.
In Guatemala there are many thieves,
and one earns very little.
So I decided to come here
to this side.
I left my wife and three children
with my family.
I write her, and the letters arrive;
yes, I know they arrive.
It is easy to return—
getting here, that is the problem.

UN VIAJE ESPANTOSO

Valentín Lucas

Fue muy sufrido el viaje
Veníamos en un trailer
y mucho calor en el trailer
Casi nos sentíamos morir
Ciento cincuenta personas
treinta y dos horas
Cubiertos y tapados
no había aire
no salía nadie para nada,
ni siquiera para ir al baño,
aguantábamos treinta y dos horas.

Hablábamos entre nosotros
que duro estaba
pero tuvimos confianza
que íbamos a llegar donde
queríamos.
Por la ambición de llegar
acá en los Estados Unidos,
tuvimos que aguantar.

Entonces
aire fresco, un pueblo chiquito
Llegamos.

A DREADFUL JOURNEY

Valentín Lucas

It was a journey of suffering
We traveled inside a trailer
lots of heat in the trailer
We almost felt we would die
A hundred and fifty people
thirty-two hours
Covered up, closed in,
no air
no one got out for anything,
not even to go to the bathroom,
we endured it for thirty-two hours.

We spoke among ourselves
about how hard it was
but we trusted
that we were going to arrive
where we were going.
Because of our ambition
to arrive here, in the United States,
we endured it.

Then
fresh air, a little town.
We arrived.

PESCANDO MANZANA EN NUEVA YORK

Braulio García González

Hoy que estoy en New York
pescando manzanas,
estoy muy contendo porque
de aquí acabando la pesca
de manzana, me voy a México
para estar con toda mi familia.
Y que lindo es para mí,
pero deseo volver
a Nueva York en enero
para contemplar la nieve.

PICKING APPLES IN NEW YORK

Braulio García González

Today I am picking apples
in New York State,
I am very content because
as soon as the apple harvest
is over, I'm going to Mexico
to be with all my family.
And how nice it is for me,
because I want to return
to New York in January
to contemplate the snow.

UN RECUERDO TRISTE

Francisca Camacho C.

Yo recuerdo que cuando me vine
de México, yo pasé por
la frontera de E.U. con mis hijos
tomando el riesgo del todo.
Yo tenía ganas de llorar y mis ojos
se ponían rojos, pero me aguanté
por mis hijos. Sólo pensaba
que dejaba mi país tan rico
y a la vez tan pobre.
Si el gobierno viera cuando
la gente se ahoga, o los matan,
o se mueren de desolación
de hambre en el camino,
no hicieran lo que hacen.
Espero que algún día se arreglan
las cosas, y no pasen más tragedias.

A SAD MEMORY

Francisca Camacho C.

I remember when I came from Mexico
I crossed over the U.S. border
with my children, risking all.
I felt like crying, and my eyes
got all red, but I held tears back
for the sake of my children.
All I thought about was that I was
leaving my country—so rich,
and at the same time so poor.
If the government could see
people suffocating, or getting killed,
dying in the desolation of hunger
on the road, they would not do
what they do.
I hope some day things will settle out
and that no more tragedies happen.

UNA HISTORIA

Joel Velásquez Pérez

Les cuento una historia de
mis padres queridos que a ellos
les pasó un caso en el año 1982.
Fue una guerra muy fuerte
fue una tierra arrasada.
Y me pongo a pensar
cuando me cuenta sus historias
porque cuando fue la guerra
mi padre vió los muertos.
El gobierno le mandó a sus
ejércitos a matar gente, campesinos,
y por esa razón mis padres viven
en una casa pobre. Apenas
pudimos conseguir el dinero
para venirme a E.U.
En el camino sufrí mucho
de hambre y otras cuestiones más.
Pero hoy que estoy en E.U.
les mandó lo poco que puedo
para que ellos puedan sobrevivir
en la casa, y ellos se sienten felices
por mí, y yo también.
Me siento orgulloso porque
ellos me ayudaron mucho.

A STORY

Joel Velásquez Pérez

I'll tell you a story
of my beloved parents, I'll tell you
what happened to them in the year 1982.
There was a hard war,
there was a devastated land.
When my father
tells these stories
I see him in the war,
coming upon the dead bodies.
The government sent in armies
to kill the people, the poor people,
which is why my parents live
in a shack. We barely
could find the money
for me to come to the U.S.
On the road I suffered from
hunger and so many other problems.
But today I am in the U.S.
I send them what little bit I can
so that they can continue to live in their shack
and they are happy
for me. I am happy, too.
I feel proud because
they helped me a lot,
now I can help them.

GUATEMALTECO

Avel Domíngues

Pues, soy un Guatemalteco
pero traigo muchas penas.
Así como yo fui un tiempo
para defender a mi patria,
pero salí de mi tiempo
y cuando llegué a mi casa
me iban a perseguir, los guerillas.
Por esa razón me vine aquí
a salvar mi vida en los E.U.,
sufriendo cansancio, hambre y sed.
Y cuando estoy en mi casa
con pena, pensando de mi familia
sin dinero para mantener mis hijos
sé que tengo que regresar
a ver a mis hijos.

GUATEMALAN

Avel Domíngues

Well, I'm a Guatemalan
I'm carrying a lot of sorrow.
I had to serve for a time
in the army, defending my country.
But when my time was up
and I arrived home
the guerillas started to persecute me.
That's why I came here,
to save my life in the U.S.,
suffering tiredness, hunger and thirst.
Now when I am in my house
I am sad, thinking of my family
without money to provide for my children
I know I have to return
to see my children.

LOS GUERILLAS

Francisco Juárez

Yo me vine de Guatemala
por los guerillas.
Pues, están matando la gente
por eso yo me vine por acá.
Vengo de un municipio,
un pueblito chiquito.
Fue una guerra entre
los guerillas y los soldados
Varios amigos míos los han matado,
vecinos míos.
De repente se puede matar a uno.
Por eso me vine por acá.
Ancianitos ya mis padres
mi padre tiene 62 años.
Me tengo que regresar a Guatemala,
para cuidarlos.

THE GUERILLAS

Francisco Juárez

I left Guatemala
because of the guerillas.
You see, they are killing the people,
that's why I came here.
I come from a region,
a tiny little town.
It was a war between
the guerillas and the soldiers.
Various friends of mine were killed,
neighbors of mine.
Suddenly I realized they might kill me.
That is why I came here.
My parents are now very old—
my father is 62 years old.
I have to return to Guatemala,
to take care of them.

RECORDANDO

Manuel Magadan B.

Escribo estas líneas
al recordar mi venida
y también al mismo tiempo
ya estoy pensado en la vida
pero eso no importa porque
sé que yo les voy a mandar dinero
a mis hijos y mi esposa Virginia
que con lágrimas en los ojos
me desea ver, esposa querida,
y escribirme seguido
yo sentía que al dejar a mi familia
dejaba un pedazo de mi vida

REMEMBERING

Manuel Magadan B.

I am writing these lines
to remember my arrival.
At the same time,
I am already thinking about my life now
but thinking about it doesn't matter—
I know I will send money
to my kids and my wife, Virginia,
who, with tears in her eyes,
desires only to see her beloved husband
and to write to me every day.
I left my family behind
I left behind a piece of my life.

TRABAJANDO

Emigdio Morales

Si ganamos poca plata acá
no se puede quedar mucho tiempo
en México. Un mes y medio
me gustaría quedar.
En las provincias me voy
a arrimar leña, para cocinar.
Tengo casa, pero comenzada
no más. Falta terminar.
Por eso quiero quedar más tiempo,
para llevar más plata para allá.
Mi última hija nació en abril.
No la conozco. Por eso quiero ir.
Por eso quiero estar tres meses
más acá, trabajando.

WORKING

Emigdio Morales

If we don't earn much money here
we can't stay long when we return
to Mexico.
I would like to stay a month and a half.
I will go to the countryside
to gather wood to cook with.
I have started to build a house,
I need to finish it.
That's why I want to stay here longer,
so I can bring more dollars back to Mexico.
My youngest daughter was born in April.
I have never seen her. Another reason why
I want to go. But I have to stay here
at least three months more, working.

VINE DE GUATEMALA

Ramiro Gómes

Yo me vine de Guatemala
por motivo que no se puede
vivir allí. Es que en mi país
hay mucha guerra, por eso
buscamos donde pasar más mejor
mi vida. Le pedí a Dios que ya
no suceden mas problemas
y yo me decidí a venir, a ganar
un dinero para mandarles
a mis papases. Y tengo que
irme para allá con ellos
para poder cuidarlos, porque
ellos se encuentran solos,
no hay quién los cuida.
No tengo más carnales. Por eso
voy a regresar.

I CAME FROM GUATEMALA

Ramiro Gómes

I came from Guatemala
because it is impossible
to live there. In my country
there is a lot of war, that's why
I looked for a better place to live
my life. I prayed to God
that nothing else would happen,
and then I decided to come here, to earn
money to send back
to my parents. Still, I have to
go back again to take care of them.
They are alone now, and there is
no one else to look after them.
I have no brothers or sisters. That
is why I will return.

LOS TIEMPOS PASADOS

Margarito Marques

Yo recuerdo aquellos años del 1960
yo andaba con mi familia trabajando.
No se me olvida los sufrimientos
que sufrímos, yo y mi familia:
la escasez de alimentos por no tener
un trabajo seguro, la falta de atención
médica a mis hijos. Ahora le doy gracias
a Dios. No estoy rico,
pero ahora ando feliz.

PAST TIMES

Margarito Marques

I remember back in the sixties
when I traveled with my family, working.
I have not forgotten how much suffering
we went through, my family and I:
lack of food, no steady work, no medical attention
for my kids. Now I give thanks
to God. I may not be rich, but
I'm happy.

UN RECUERDO

Artémio Morales Díaz

En el poblado Nuevo Amatenango,
municipio de Amatenango, allí vivo.
Compré un sitio con una casa
y la casa faltaba servicio de agua
y de luz
pero yo ya lo instalé, yo y mi esposa,
y logré hacer esto por hacer
un dinerito.

Ahora la tengo enmayado con hierro
para proteger que no entran ladrones,
también tengo una esquinita allá
frente a la carretera, con jardín.

Tengo flores, buganvilla, tulipán,
y muchas flores de todos los colores,
pero la buganvilla es de color guinda.
la tengo armada con alhambre
para que sube las paredes en frente.

Cada año trabajo aquí
para no sufrir en tierras ajenas
cuando tengo cincuenta años,
volvere allí donde tengo todo.

A MEMORY

Artémio Morales Díaz

In the little village of Nuevo Amatenango,
in the municipality of Amatenango, I lived.
I bought a site with a house
and the house had no water
or electric
but I installed it, me and my wife,
and I managed to do this by making
a little money.

Now it's fenced in with wire
so that thieves can't enter.
Also, I have a little corner place facing
the highway, with a garden.

I have flowers—bouganvillea, tulips,
many flowers, all colors,
the bouganvillea is plum colored.
I have it strung up with wire
so it climbs the walls in front.

Every year I work here ensures
I will not have to suffer in foreign lands
when I am fifty years old—
I will be in Nuevo Amantenango,
where I have everything.

RECUERDO DE MI INFANCIA

Martín Mendoza

Recuerdo mi infancia
y a mi memoria se viene la pobreza
de mi gente,
al yo querer salir adelante
y tener la impotencia ante mí.
Sentí desesperación al sentirme
un niño y no poder hacer nada.
Ahora que han pasado los años
veo poco a poco la superación
y oigo la felicidad en la voz de mi familia,
al escucharlos me siento conforme
sabiendo que se encuentran todos con bien.
Toco mis manos y aunque maltratadas
me siento verdaderamente feliz
al saber que mi esfuerzo no ha sido en vano,
y le doy gracias a Dios por lo que me ha dado,
y también por lo que me ha quitado.

A MEMORY OF MY CHILDHOOD

Martín Mendoza

I remember my childhood,
the poverty
of my people,
wanting to get ahead,
powerless to do so.
I felt desperate as a child,
unable to do anything.
Now years have passed,
I see little by little I've passed these feelings,
I hear the happy voices
of my family, and
I feel satisfied knowing they are all well
I clasp my hands, and though they are battered
I feel truly happy
knowing my effort has not been in vain.
I thank God for what He has given me,
and also for what He has taken away.

VENIR POR POBREZA

Ademar Pérez Gálvez

Yo vivía en el campo
con sierra, sierra baja
y bosque también hay.
Pero no se puede cultivar
la tierra,
por ejemplo, no puede cultivar
café ni algodón
porque la tierra no da.
Por eso existe la pobreza.
Yo y mis padres
hicimos la lucha
para que yo viniera acá
para poder vivir mejor
con toda la familia.
A salir de mi casa, he pasado
por desiertos, sufriendo mucho
por la decisión
por llegar a los Estados Unidos.
Ahora que estoy aquí
les mando dinero
para que se mantengan.
Y el día que yo regreso
les haré muy felices.

BECAUSE OF POVERTY

Ademar Pérez Gálvez

I lived in a country
with mountains, low mountains
and there are also forests.
But you cannot cultivate
the land.
For example, you cannot grow
coffee or cotton
because the earth does not give.
That is why poverty exists.
My parents and I
struggled together
so that I could come here
and live better
for my whole family.
To leave my home, I crossed
deserts, I suffered a lot
because of my decision
to come to the United States.
Now that I am here
I send them money
so they can support themselves.
And the day that I return
they will be even happier.

UNA PEQUEÑA TRISTEZA

Jaime Márquez

Una pequeña tristeza
que todavía tengo en la mente,
cuando yo venía para los Estados Unidos.
Pasamos mucho cansancio, sed, frío,
y sueño, y por fin llegué aquí,
y estoy muy a gusto.

Lo que más extraño de mi tierra,
que es México,
es el olor de las flores bonitas
que están en mi casa.
Y por la mañana el oír
como cantan los gallos.

A LITTLE SADNESS

Jaime Márquez

A little sadness still in my mind
about when I came to the United States.
We endured tiredness, thirst,
cold and lack of sleep.
And at last we arrived here,
and it's much to my liking.

What I miss most about my homeland,
which is Mexico,
is the smell of the pretty flowers
at my house.
And in the mornings, to hear
the cocks crow.

DÍA DE LOS MUERTOS

Celso Trejo

Es un aniversario
El mes de los muertitos
El mes de ánimas,
El Segundo de Noviembre

Toda la familia está
todos los familiares,
hacen tamales, y café
Hemos ido a la misa a mediodía,
el costumbre del Día de los Muertos
Cada año.

Mi mujer, mis cinco hijos
mis padres, mis hermanas,
todos estamos sentados
estamos rezando cantos
para los muertos,
en el olor de las velas
en la mesa.

DAY OF THE DEAD

Celso Trejo

It's an anniversary
The month of the dearly departed
The month of the spirits
The Second of November

The whole family is there,
all the relations,
they make tamales and coffee
We've gone to Midday Mass,
a custom of the Day of the Dead
each year.

My wife, my five children,
my parents, my sisters
we're all seated
reciting prayers
for the dead
in the smell of the candles
on the table.

RECUERDOS DE MI PUEBLO

Procopio González

En abril, cuando salí de mi pueblo
salí medio pensativo de mi familia
andaba medio mal de la cabeza
por andar pensativo.

Al llegar acá no había trabajo
pasé un mes sin trabajo.

Tengo allí toda la familia,
mi esposa, mis tres hijos,
nuestra casa propia en el pueblo.

Tengo muchos árboles—
mangos, aguacates, flores y plantas,
y unas plantas que huelen bonitas.

Aquí cuando nieve para mí es extraño
prefiero el calor.
Donde vivo cerca a Acapulco
hace mucho calor.

MEMORIES OF MY VILLAGE

Procopio González

In April, I left my village
I left preoccupied with my family
I walked around with a headache
from thinking so much.

On arriving here, there was no job
I went a month without working.

Everyone in my family is still there,
my wife, my three kids,
in our own house in the village.

I have many trees—
mangos, avocados, flowers and
plants, some plants that smell pretty.

Here when it snows, it is strange for me
I prefer heat.
Where I live, near Acapulco,
it is very hot.

LOS AMIGOS NO MIENTEN

Alfonzo Saenz

Hace diez años yo empecé a plantar
pinos en el estado de Louisiana.
Allá tengo muchos amigos
que me ayudan a terminar de plantar.
Cada día que pasaba venían a ayudarme
mis amigos, los armadillos.
Mis amigos vivían en la sierra.
Ellos me esperaban con ansiedad
en unos agujeros que ellos mismos
hacían en que yo les echara puños
y puños de pinos para que
ellos comieran y al mismo tiempo
yo terminar mi trabajo.
Digo mis amigos porque
ellos a nadie le decían nada.
Pero porque ellos no hablan
es por eso digo
verdaderos amigos!

FRIENDS DON'T LIE

Alfonzo Saenz

Ten years ago I began planting
pines in the state of Louisiana
There I have many friends
who helped me finish planting.
Every day they came to help me
my friends, the armadillos.
My friends lived in the mountains.
They waited for me anxiously
in holes they had dug
in which I would throw handfuls
of pine seeds, some of which they ate,
but some of which grew.
The armadillos helped me to finish
my work more quickly.
I call them my friends because
they never said anything to anyone.
Well, that's because they don't talk
and that's why I call them
my true friends!

UN RECUERDO DE MI NIÑEZ

Roberto Gómez

Yo vengo de la ciudad más grande
del mundo, la capital, y mi barrio
es un pueblo chiquito.
Nada más me gustaba que jugar
fútbol con mis amigos en el llano.
Jugábamos todos los domingos.

Y había un profesor que odiaba
porque nos pegaba mucho,
porque no aprendíamos
o porque no hicimos la tarea.
Nos golpeaba en las manos.
Era un gordo y alto
y nos pegaba mucho.

Sin embargo me gustó la escuela
porque allí aprendí a leer
y escribir.
Y mi amigo Martín y yo
jugábamos mucho, saliendo
en las tardes.

A MEMORY FROM MY CHILDHOOD

Roberto Gómez

I come from the biggest city in the world,
the capital, and my neighborhood
is a little village.
There was nothing I liked more than playing
soccer on the field with my friends.
We played every Sunday.

There was a teacher I hated
because he hit us a lot,
because we weren't learning
or we didn't do our homework.
He hit us on our hands.
He was a tall fat man
and he hit us a lot.

Still, I liked school
because I learned to read
and write there.
And I played a lot
with my friend Martin, when we left
in the afternoons.

RECUERDO DE MI AMIGA

Maricela Meza Camacho

Me recuerdo cuando tú y yo fuimos
a la escuela, y cuando tú y yo
jugábamos de pequeñitas.
También recuerdo cuando tú y yo
nos ayudábamos una a la otra.
Yo tenía que ir a otro pueblo.
Pero aún así todavía te recuerdo
de vez en cuando.
Yo quisiera verte sonriendo
una vez más.

MEMORY OF MY FRIEND

Maricela Meza Camacho

I remember when you and I went
to school, when you and I
played together as little kids.
I remember too when you and I
helped each other.
I had to move to another town.
But even so I still remember you
from time to time.
I would like to see you smiling
one more time.

CUANDO VOY A MI PUEBLITO

Artemio Covarrubias Chávez

Hidalgo de mi niñez fue un pueblito
de la sierra, olía a flores,
plantas y frutas
su clima templado, había naranjas
guayabas, y higos.

Tenemos animales—vacas y gallinas
y patos,
y sus sonidos en la mañana
de los pájaros y los burros, la brisa
corría despacio como una tortuga.

En el ranchito se comen tortillas
de maíz que hace mi mamá,
con caldo de pollo, frijoles y arroz.

Me acuerdo más mi mamá,
su cabello negro, su sonrisa feliz
su mirada tranquila cuando llego yo.

WHEN I GO TO MY VILLAGE

Artemio Covarrubias Chávez

Hidalgo of my childhood! A little town
in the mountains. It smelled of flowers,
plants and fruit.
It had a temperate climate,
oranges, and guavas, and figs.

We have animals—cows and chickens
and ducks,
and the sounds in the morning
of the birds and the burros, the breeze
flowing slowly as a turtle.

At the ranch we eat corn tortillas
that my mother makes,
chicken soup, beans, and rice.

Mostly I remember my mother,
her black hair, her happy smile,
her tranquil glance when I arrive.

MI CANASTA

Margarita Sierra

Mamita me ha dicho
que Dios me mandó
en esta canasta
que aquí tengo yo

Un angel la trajo
vestida de azul
un angel del cielo
no lo viste tú

Mil mariposita
vinieron con él
y mil pajaritos
vinieron también

Canasta llena
de rosas y solo
canasta en que vine
dormidita yo

¿Y saben lo que
he visto yo?¡

Que en mi canasta
compran el pan!

MY BASKET

Margarita Sierra

My mother told me
that God sent me
in this basket
I have here

An angel brought it
dressed in blue
an angel from the sky
unseen by you

A thousand butterflies
came with him
and a thousand small birds
came too

Basket full
of roses and alone
basket that I came in
sleepy one

And you know what
I see now instead?
They're using my birth-basket
to buy bread!

A MI MADRE

Abelino Velásquez H.

Madre querida,
hoy me acuerdo de ti
porque me encuentro muy lejos de ti.
Espero que ojalá madre mía
se acuerde de mí,
que ojalá Dios nos cuide a nosotros
y a muchos más que se encuentran
igual que nosotros
lejos de nuestra patria.
Gracias.

TO MY MOTHER

Abelino Velásquez H.

Beloved mother,
I remember you today
Though I am far far far away.
I hope mother of mine
that you remember me,
I hope that God will care for us
and the many others who
like us
are far from their homeland.
Gracias.

LA MUERTE DE MI MADRE

Guadalupe Sánchez

Cuando mi mama se murió
yo la miraba
me sentí tan inútil
mirar aquellas manos
que tanto me había acariciado.
Yo miraba que ella respiraba
se me hacía que en cualquier
momento me iba hablar.
El tiempo pasó y siguió
dormida.
Cuando la llevamos al cementerio
sentía un frío que me consumía.
¿Como era posible que la
fuéramos a dejar allí sola?
Hacía mucho frío
y después llovió.
Yo pensaba que ella sentía
que iba a decir que mis hijos
son tan ingratos.
Desde este momento
me recuerdo siempre y siento
una profunda tristeza.
Esto pasó en Diciembre, 1995.
Desde entonces
no he tenido una Navidad.

MY MOTHER'S DEATH

Guadalupe Sánchez

When my mother died
I looked at her
and felt so useless
looking at those hands
that had caressed me.
It seemed as I looked that she was breathing,
it seemed that at any moment
she was going to speak to me.
Time passed and still
she slept.
When we carried her to the cemetery
I felt a cold consume me.
How could we
leave her all alone?
It was very cold
and then, it rained.
I could almost hear her say
My children
are so ungrateful.
I remember that moment
It always causes me
a profound sadness.
This happened in December, 1995.
Since then
I have not had a Christmas.

MI MADRE

Martín Mendoza

Mi madre tuvo cuatro hijos
de los cuales a todos quiso
por igual; los cuidó como
solo ella supo hacerlo.
Por principio los enseñó
a caminar, hablar, comer, etc.
Después de su tarea comenzada
los fue educando poco a poco
y encaminando hacia
la vida correcta.
Todo esto fue hecho
con el amor de madre
que todo ser humano o animal
ofrece a un hijo, y ya su tarea
terminada, los echó a volar
hacia la vida
con el mismo amor
que les educó.

MY MOTHER

Martín Mendoza

My mother had four children
she loved equally;
she took care of them
as only she knew how to.
To start with, she taught them
to walk, to talk, to eat, etc.
After this work had begun
she started educating them,
little by little, and walking them
toward a correct life.
All this was done
with a mother's love
that every human being, every animal
offers to her child. Now that her work
was complete, she cast them up to fly
toward life
with the same love
that had trained them.

CUANDO FALLECIÓ MI ABUELA

María Teresa Flores

Cuando vivíamos en Brockport, era
el primer año que vinimos para acá
a trabajar, y teníamos muy poquito
dinero. Y luego a nosotros nos hablaron
por teléfono, y yo tuve que contestar.
Era una mala noticia—que mi abuela
acaba de morir. Y fue muy triste
porque nosotros no podíamos ir
hasta México porque estaba muy
lejos, y no hablábamos suficiente
inglés, y no teníamos mucho dinero.

WHEN MY GRANDMOTHER DIED

María Teresa Flores

We lived in Brockport. It was
the first year we came here to work,
and we had very little money.
We got a telephone call,
and I had to answer.
It was bad news—my grandmother
had died. And it was so sad
because we couldn't go to Mexico
because it was too far, and we
didn't speak enough English,
and we didn't have enough money.

UN POEMA TRISTE

Rómulo Bernardo Cortez

Caminando en los campos
del castilo del gran rey
vino a mi mente un rayo
de recuerdos de repente

El teléfono que timbra
hace un momento varias
veces
tengo miedo de contestar
pues presiento lo que quieren

Amigos y gente que no conozco
elevan rezos y cantos
mientras familiares lloran
tristes y amargamente

¡Cuántas flores hay en la sala!
Yo creo que tú nunca
habías visto tantas
Madre, ¿por qué no me can-
tas?

Te has quedado callada
con tus ojos hermosos
entreabiertos y tu blanca
dentadura no muestra más

Tu blanca piel
se ha puesto tan pálida
ya no hay diferencia
entre las velas y
las flores de la sala

La última vez que nos vimos
hablamos de tantas cosas
y te quedaste esperando mi
regreso
tal vez en el mes de enero

Madre, por favor despierta
que ya los vecinos se acercan
con flores en las manos
y encendidas las velas

A SAD POEM

Rómulo Bernardo Cortez

Walking in the fields
of the castle of the great king
a flash of memory comes
suddenly to mind

The telephone that rang
several times a moment ago
I am afraid to answer
I can guess what they want

Friends and people I don't
know
raise their voices in prayer
and songs
while the family members cry
sadly and bitterly

How many flowers in the living room!
I believe that you have never
seen so many
Mother, why don't you sing to
me?

You keep silent
with your beautiful eyes
half opened and your white
denture you will never show
again

Your white skin
has become so pale
there is no difference now
between the candles
and the flowers in the room

The last time we saw each
other
we spoke of so many things
and you were awaiting my
return
perhaps in the month of
January

Mother, please wake up
the neighbors are approaching
with flowers in their hands
and lit candles

POEMA AL MOJADO

Carlos Vargas

Cuando salí de Morelos
a los Estados Unidos
con mucha tristeza
dejé a mi familia y mi pueblo
por buscar una vida mejor.
Sin saber encontraría lo peor.

Es por eso que me acuerdo
a mi pueblo y me invade la tristeza
y me dan ganas de llorar.
Pero no puedo.
Por no acobardarme yo sólo.

Porque vine a sufrir
para poder salir sacar adelante
mi familia y darles una vida mejor.

WETBACK POEM

Carlos Vargas

It was with great sadness
that I left Morelos
to go to the United States.
I left my family and my village
to seek a better life.
Not knowing I would find one even worse.

It is because of this I remember
my village and sadness invades me
and makes me want to cry.
But I cannot.
I will not be intimidated by myself.

I suffer here in order
to bring my family forward,
to give them a better life.

TRABAJO

Natividad Almanza

Pues, para empezar, vengo de México
en busca de trabajo.
La primera vez fue en '71,
pero me deportaron.
Pasaron 13 años para después
regresar de nuevo.
Mi casa es en Tlaxcala,
allí la gente en las provincias
hablan un dialecto, pero yo, no.
Mi mujer y mis ocho hijos
los tenía allá. Tres de ellos
están ahora en New Jersey
para trabajar. Vinieron escondidos.
Pero no estamos en contacto
desde que vengo de Miami.
De todo el trabajo me gusta más
el blueberry en New Jersey
porque están el tamaño de uno
y fácil a pizcar.

WORK

Natividad Almanza

Well, to begin with, I came from Mexico
in search of work.
The first time was in '71,
but they deported me.
Thirteen years passed before I
returned again.
My house is in Tlaxcala.
There in the provinces the people
speak another dialect, but not me.
My wife and my eight children
were there. Now three
of them are working in New Jersey.
They came in on the sly.
But we are not in contact since
I got here from Miami.
Of all the work I like best
picking the blueberries in New Jersey
because the bushes are the same size
as me, and easy to pick.

LA SEGUNDA VEZ

Lorenzo Martínez

Yo pasé por Tijuana al otro lado
pero me agarraron cuando crucé la línea
y me encerraron en unos
cuartos enormes.
Éramos más de trescientos
alli estuvimos toda la noche.
Hacía mucho calor, pero aguantamos;
casi queremos ahogar.
Pero el otro día nos echaron para fuera
hasta llegar a Tijuana.
Pero el otro día nos regresamos
y nos volvímos a pasar por la línea.
Entonces ellos no nos agarraron,
y fuimos a llegar hasta Watsonville,
California. Allí trabajábamos pero
ganabamos muy poco, y tuvimos
que buscar otro trabajo donde pudimos
ganar más dinero. Por fin estuvimos
contentos!

THE SECOND TIME

Lorenzo Martínez

I passed through Tijuana to the other side
but they grabbed me up when I crossed the line
and they locked me up in some
huge rooms.
We were more than three hundred
there all night long.
It was very hot, but we put up with it;
we almost drowned from the heat.
The next day they threw us back
all the way to Tijuana.
The day after that we returned
and came back over the border.
This time they didn't grab us,
and we travelled until we reached Watsonville,
California. There we worked, but
we earned very little, so we had to
find a job where they would
pay us more money. Finally,
we were content!

TRES AVENTURAS

Santiago Marques

Cuando yo tenía dieciséis años
fue mi primera aventura
en la frontera de Matamoros;
bueno, comoquiera, yo caminé
toda la noche.
La segunda vez en Laredo
yo ya tenía veinte años.
La tercera vez en Nogales, Arizona,
habían víboras en el desierto,
yo llevaba mi galón de agua,
y yo iba con dos amigos—
muy buena gente—
Bueno, esta vez llegamos
hasta el estado de Montana.
Había mucha nieve, hasta en May
y mucho frío.

MY THREE ADVENTURES

Santiago Marques

When I was sixteen years old
I had my first adventure.
It was on the frontier in Matamoros;
oh yes, but I had to walk
all night.
The second time, in Laredo,
I was twenty years old.
And the third time, in Nogales,
there were snakes in the desert.
I carried my gallon of water,
and I went with two friends—
very good people—
Well, that time we got as far
as the state of Montana.
There was a lot of snow, even in May,
and it was very cold.

EL VIAJE

Antonio López

Yo me vine de mi casa
de Guatemala
Aquí me vine por pobreza
por no tener dinero
Pasé por desiertos de Los E. U.
sufrí mucha hambre
Habían muchos de nosotros
pero cuatro no más seguíamos
Vine acá no más para ganar
un dinero
En el desierto caminaba ocho días,
sin comida, sin agua.

THE JOURNEY

Antonio López

I came from my home
in Guatemala
I came here because of poverty
because of having no money
I crossed the deserts of United States
I suffered a lot of hunger
There were many of us
but only four of us kept on
I came here only to earn
some money
In the desert I walked eight days,
without food, without water.

RECUERDO DE UN TIEMPO PASADO

Platón Márquez

Me nombraron Platón por un abuelo
que yo tenía.
Él vivía en el estado de Querétaro.

Yo, mi hermano, y mi papá
estábamos trabajando en una milpa
para sembrar maíz. Todo el día
estábamos allí, fue el mes de junio.

Hemos llevado frijoles, tortillas,
un poquito de carne, también,
y agua para tomar.
Como trabajábamos lejos,
nos íbamos diario. Grande fue la milpa,
de la casa dos o tres horas a caminar.

Cuando llegamos a la casa
allí estaba la comida.
nos dormíamos
para el otro día irnos.

MEMORY OF A PAST TIME

Platón Márquez

They named me Plato for a grandfather
that I had.
He lived in the state of Queretaro.

Me, my brother, and my father
were working in a field
planting corn. All day
we were there, it was in the month of June.

We brought beans, tortillas,
a little meat, also,
and water to drink.
Since we were working far from home,
we set out every morning. The field was large,
a two or three hours' walk from home.

When we returned home
there was a meal.
We went right to sleep
to go out again the next day.

POEMA SIN TÍTULO

Humberto Hernández

Una mañana mordió la tierra
La nieve aún cubriá
El sol parecía tener frió
Era un bello amanecer de invierno

Sentí tu mirada, mas verte no podía.
Oculto bajo la nieve estabas,
Tal vez miedo de mi tendrías.

Cotidiano trabajo empecé.
Murmullos de voces se escuchaban
Comentarios, logré encontrar con sorpresa
Tan solo ramas bajo la nieve
Mis manos te tocaron
Algo electrizante por mi cuerpo recorría.

Mis brazos abrí a diferentes árboles
En mis hombros los llevé.
Al campo a sembrar, me fui.
Con cariño te planté,
Porque eres especialmente diferente.

Nuevemente en la primavera
Nos encontramos, y ¡me recuerdas!
Con asombro te acaricio, a ti parecía agradarte.
¡Yo sabía que eres especial!
Amigos por siempre prometimos.

Tu altivéz y elegancia aún conservas
En tus ramas las aves,
Con sus trinos de alegría.
En tu fresca sombra, murmullos de enamorados.
¿Cuántas promesas de amor
Y secretos guardarás?

No recuerdo rey alguno vestirse de la manera.
El sol ilumina tus hojas de colores diferentes
Coronarte como rey en pleno verano y primavera.
El tiempo transcurre en su presuroso paso al futuro
Amigo mío, estás diferente, y yo también
Porque en otoño estamos.

Tu altivéz y elegancia aún conservas
En tus ramas las aves,
Con sus trinos de alegría.
En tu fresca sombra, murmullos de enamorados.
¿Cuántas promesas de amor
Y secretos guardarás?

El invierno presuroso se acerca
Dormirás bajo la nieve
Como cuando apenas eras una rama
¿Me recordarás?
¿Recordarás este viejo que te sembró
Que cuidó de ti?
¿Y qué en el ardiente verano te regó
Con el sudor de su esfuerzo
Y agua de manantial?

Veo tus hojas caer in abundancia como lágrimas
Acaso presientes nuestra despedida.
En verdad, yo también estoy triste.
Yo acepto nuestra separación.

Me llevaré tus semillas
Las cultivaré en el huerto de mi alma
Y te regaré con mi cariño.
Tendrás calor de mi amor
Y estarás custodiadocon mi corazón,
Junto con las estaciones del año.
Y no hará más dolores ni tristes
Despedidas.¡ Viejos amigos,
Mi árbol y yo!

UNTITLED POEM

Humberto Hernández

Morning etched the earth
Snow still covering the ground
The sun seemed to be chilled
It was a beautiful winter's dawn.

I felt your glance, but couldn't see you,
Hidden beneath the snow
Perhaps afraid of me.

I began my daily work.
Murmuring voices were heard gossiping
Surprised, I found
Branches so alone under the snow
My hands touched you
Something electrifying ran through my body.

I opened my arms to a bundle of saplings
I carried them on my shoulder
To plant them in the field.
I made sure to plant you with love
You are so special.

Next springtime
We find each other, and you remember me
With amazement I caress you. You seem to like it.
I knew you were special!
We promise to be friends forever.

In your pride and elegance you even care for
The birds trilling joy
Among your branches.
In your cool shade, lovers' whispers are heard.
How many promises of love
And secrets will you keep?

I can't remember any king dressed in such a manner.
The sun illuminates your multicolored leaves,
Crowns you king between spring and summer.
Time passes in its frantic passage to the future.
My friend, you are different, and so am I
Because now we are in autumn.

In your pride and elegance you even care for
The birds trilling joy
Among your branches.
In your cool shade, lovers' whispers are heard.
How many promises of love
And secrets will you keep?

Winter is approaching so quickly
When you sleep beneath the snow
Just as when you were only a sapling
Will you remember me?
Will you remember this old man who planted you,
Who took care of you,
And who in the flaming summer watered you
With the sweat of his strength
And the water from the well?

I see your leaves fall in abundance like tears
Perhaps you are already anticipating our goodbye.
In truth, I am also sad.
I accept our separation.

I will take your seeds with me
I will plant them in the garden of my heart
And I will water you with my love.
You will be warmed by my love
And you will be watched over by my heart,
Along with the seasons of the year.
And there won't be any more pain or sad
Goodbyes. Old friends,
My tree and I!

GOTA DE AGUA

Rómulo Bernardo Cortez

Me ves tan indefensa
transparente y diáfana
porque por ahora
tan solo soy una gota de agua.

Pero no siempre soy así
Ah no, a veces cuando
logro unirme a mis demás
hermanas soy tan diferente.

Cuando soy río, voy
serpenteando entre valles
montes y praderas
y no hay nada que
me detenga.

Como la voz del corazón
enamorado, así formo
cascadas de estrepitosa
voz ensordecedora.

Otras veces formo
lagos donde reina la quietud
y sirvo la inspiración
a todo artista desde su juventud.

Hay tantas cosas que soy
pero por ahora tan sólo
una gota de agua cristalina,
un diamante que el cielo te regala.

Perdona, por favor, mi nostalgia,
y llévame al contorno de tus labios
y convierte esta simple gota
en el diamante húmedo
de un tierno beso.

DROP OF WATER

Rómulo Bernardo Cortez

You see me so defenseless,
transparent and diaphanous
because for now
I am but one drop of water.

But I am not always like this
Ah no, sometimes when
I succeed in joining my other
sisters I am very different.

When I am a river I go
meandering through valleys
mountains and meadows
and nothing
can detain me.

I am the voice of the heart
in love. In this way, I form
waterfalls with a resounding
deafening voice.

Other times I form
lakes where stillness reigns
and I serve the inspiration
of every artist from their youth.

There are so many things I am
but for now I am only
a crystalline drop of water,
a diamond the sky gives you.

Please pardon my nostalgia,
and take me to the contour of your lips
and convert this simple drop
into the moist diamond
of a tender kiss.

DOS BRUJAS

Hosvaldo Mejía

Una vez fuimos en la noche de cacería,
mis amigos y yo,
caminábamos bastante por las praderas
no había animales para cazar,
y seguímos caminando hacia un arroyo
grande con dos cuervos
que se levantaban
Nos quedamos mudos de miedo.
Eran dos brujas soltando luces
como platillos voladores.
Corrímos y corrímos hasta llegar a casa.

TWO WITCHES

Hosvaldo Mejía

One time we went hunting at night,
my friends and I, we walked
and walked through the fields
but there were no animals to hunt.
We kept on walking toward a big
ravine when two crows
flew up.
We were struck dumb with fear.
They were two witches, throwing off
light like flying saucers.
We ran and ran until we reached home.

LA SOMBRA

Gerardo Ramírez Yánez

Una vez, caminando por la noche,
venía con unos botes de agua
y al pasar frente a la iglesia
del pueblo, sentí mucho miedo.
No sabía por qué, pero
no se me quitaba.
Y al querer pasar una cerca de piedra
levanté la vista, y frente a mí
estaba una sombra en la forma
de un burro que se movía
y crecía más y más.
¡Pero no había burro!
Enseguida me alcanzó un amigo
que me dijo, "¿Qué tienes?"
Porque me vío asustado.
Le plactiqué lo que me había pasado
y le dió por reírse de mí,
deciéndome que yo estaba loco.

THE SHADOW

Gerardo Ramírez Yánez

One time, walking at night,
I was carrying some jars of water,
and passing in front of the church
of the village, I was suddenly afraid.
I didn't know why, but
it wouldn't leave me.
And as I was passing a stone wall
I raised my eyes, and right in front of me
was a shadow in the form
of a burro that moved
and grew larger.
But there was no burro!
At once a friend caught up with me
and said, "What's the matter?"
because he saw me so scared.
I told him what had happened
and he started to laugh at me,
telling me that I was crazy.

LEYENDA MAYA LA X-TABAY

José Maoro C.

Allá por los pueblos antiguos
Donde existen las haciendas antiguas
Hay unas matas, unos árboles
Llamados *ceíbo*
Cuentan los antiguos que
Entrando la noche si pasa un hombre
A ese lugar, aparece una mujer chula,
Muy hermosa, bien peinada,
Bien arreglada
Seduce a los hombres que pasan allá.
Embruja a los hombres con sus
Encantos, y después se los domina
Ellos pierden su voluntad
Y hacen lo que ella dice
Los lleva a su cueva
Y los mata
Esas personas no regresan
Se llama X-Tabay

MAYAN LEGEND OF X-TABAY

José Maoro C.

There in the ancient villages
Where the old properties are
There are shrubs—a kind of tree
Called *ceíbo*
The old people say that when night
Enters, if a man passes that place,
A wild woman appears—
Very beautiful, flashily dressed,
Her hair beautifully combed
She seduces the men who pass that way,
She bewitches them with her charms,
And then she subdues them.
They lose their will
and they do what she says.
She brings them to her cave
And kills them.
Those guys won't return
Her name is X-Tabay!

UN ESPANTO

Maclovio Covarrubias

Cuando yo era muy chiquillo
me gustaba mucho salir solo al campo
al trabajo, pero una vez hice
un capricho, y renegando
salí para mi labor. Al ir caminando
por el camino pensaba en que algo
malo me podía pasar.
De repente, al entrar a mi labor
oí algo como un quejido
y que me regresé corriendo
para mi casa.
Pero como yo iba caminando
por el camino, algo iba siguiéndome
por abajo del camino.
No pude ver a nadie, solamente
que la hierba se iba moviendo
como si algo trataba de ganarme el paso,
y desde entonces empezé a sentir miedo
salir solo al campo

A FRIGHT

Maclovio Covarrubias

When I was little, I used to love
to walk alone through the fields
to work, but one day on a whim
I started cursing and swearing
on my way to work. On the road
I thought something bad
was going to happen.
Suddenly, as I got to the job
I heard something like a low moan
and I turned to run back
to my house.
But as I ran along the road
something was following me
below the road.
I couldn't see anyone, but
the grass was moving
as if something were running after me,
trying to catch me!
And since then I have begun to feel fear
walking through the fields alone.

ABURRIDO

Balbino Silverio

De diez y nueve días aquí y hemos
trabajado cinco, a causa de la lluvia.
Estamos como en la cárcel
pues, que no pasa nadie por aquí,
ni una mosca.
No tenemos dirección. Nadie sabe
llegar aquí. El vecino está aquí
dos años. Tampoco tiene dirección.

No podemos conseguir
una muchacha
para quitar el mal pensamiento
que tiene uno.
Solamente si uno tiene mujer
uno puede tranquilizarse.
Mejor que hablar de eso
o del otro
es platicar con ella.

BORED

Balbino Silverio

Nineteen days here and we have
worked only five, because of the rain.
Well, it is like we are in jail—
no one passes by,
not even a fly.
We have no address. No one knows
how to get here. Our neighbor has been here
two years. He has no address, either.

We can't find
a girlfriend
to take away the bad thoughts.
Only a woman
can make a man calm.
Better than speaking of this
or of that
is speaking with her.

NO MÁS MUERTE

Jaime Trejo

Que no te perturbe la sombra de la duda.
Pues tu sonrisa es mi sonrisa. Tu llanto
es mi llanto. Tu alma es mi alma, y tu
corazón es mi corazón. ¿Cómo pues podría
destrozar mi alma y matar mi corazón?
No hay tiempo para la tristeza, pues
el mundo es un suspiro, mas nuestro amor
es para siempre. Deja que fluja el río, que
nada te quite el sueño. Pues ni la muerte
podrá arrancar el amor. Es más fuerte
el amor que la muerte. La muerte es solo
del cuerpo, mas el alma permanece.
Cultivemos nuestro amor que ningún
vendaval borre nuestra sonrisa.
Donde hay amor está Dios, y donde
está Dios no falta nada. No te envenenes,
pues el mundo está lleno de ponzoña.
Mas si tienes a Dios contigo nada podrá
contra ti. No temas caer. ¡Pues Dios
te sostiene con mano firme!

NO MORE DEATH

Jaime Trejo

Don't let the shadow of doubt perturb you.
Your smile is my smile. Your crying,
my crying. Your soul is my soul, and your
heart is my heart. How then could anyone
destroy my soul, kill my heart?
There is no time for sadness— the world
is just a sigh, but our love is for always.
Let the river flow, let nothing
take away the dream. Not even death
can uproot love. Love is stronger
than death. Death is only of the body,
but the soul remains.
Let's grow our love so no
wind can erase our smile.
Where there is love, there is God,
and where God is, nothing is lacking.
Don't poison yourself, the world is full enough
of venom. If God is with you,
everything is with you. Don't worry about
falling, God supports you with a steady hand!

EN UN INSTANTE

Rómulo Bernardo Cortez

Hace ya varios años
que soñe te vi un instante
y solo te ví un instante
para después, seguir
soñando nuevemente.

Las ideas se revuelan
en mi mente y corazón
como paros dormidos
temerosos del viento

Las mariposas que juegan
a hacer el amor, en una
flor que estaba muriendo
sin marchitar su color
amarillo.

Las mariposas que juegan
a hacer el amor
mientras los pájaros
estan dormidos.

Una montaña que juega
con el atardecer
es un mundo nuevo, igual
que tus ojos verde claro

Y qué decir de la música
de tus labios.

Para decir te quiero
con un instante basta,
para decir te amo
la eternidad no alcanza.

Qué me importa
lo que tiene sentido,
si en cada frase que dices
encuentro un poema
que aún no escribo

A los pájaros dormidos
los has lanzado al vuelo
y revolotean en mi corazón
como verdaderos pájaros
en celo.

IN AN INSTANT

Rómulo Bernardo Cortez

Several years ago
I dreamt I knew you
I saw you only an instant
and afterward continued
dreaming

Ideas turn around
in my mind and heart
like sleeping birds
afraid of the wind

Butterflies play
at making love
inside a dying flower
whose yellow color
is unfading.

The butterflies play
at making love
while the birds
are asleep.

A mountain that plays
with the late afternoon
is a new world, equal
to your light green eyes

And what to say of the music
from your lips.

To say I want you
one instant suffices
to say I love you
eternity is not enough time.

What do I care
what makes sense,
if in each phrase you speak
I find a poem
I still don't write

You have hurled into flight
the sleeping birds
and they flap in my heart
like real birds
in heat.

ANGÉLICA

Manuel Vásquez

¿Mi novia?
Yo luché cinco años por ella
noviando con ella
conquistándola

Angélica,
yo yendo a mirarla
todas las noches,
Ella es morena, alta, cabello lacio
largo, sus ojos color café.

Salimos a campo en caballo
los dos en mi caballo,
como un paseo
por Santa Clara, mi rancho.

Fue la primavera,
había el olor de los árboles,
los grillos estaban chiflando,
la sonrisa de Angélica como la luna
creciente.

ANGELICA

Manuel Vásquez

My girlfriend?
I fought five years for her—
courting her,
winning her over.

Angelica!
Going to see her
every night—
Brown skinned, tall, hair
long and straight, eyes
the color of coffee.

We went to the countryside
on horseback
the two of us, together on my horse
going for a ride through Santa Clara, my settlement.

It was spring,
there was the smell of the trees,
the crickets whistling, Angelica's
smile like the growing moon.

RECORDÁNDOTE

Emilio Rodríguez Trejo

Hoy pensé en ti
como siempre lo hago
y te encontré en lo más
profundo de mi ser

A veces me encuentro triste
y pensando en ti
todo me alegra la vida
cualquier cosa—una flor,
una piedra—todo

Hoy pensé en ti
como siempre lo haré
porque por ti vivo
y por ti viviré

REMEMBRANCE

Emilio Rodríguez Trejo

Today I thought of you
like I always do
and I found you
in the deepest part of my being

Sometimes I find myself sad—
and thinking of you
everything makes my life happy
a flower,
a stone—everything.

Today I thought of you
like I always do
because I live for you
like I always will do.

Breinigsville, PA USA
03 December 2009
228453BV00001B/23/A